GET INVOLVED!

ANIMAL RIGHTS ACTIVIST

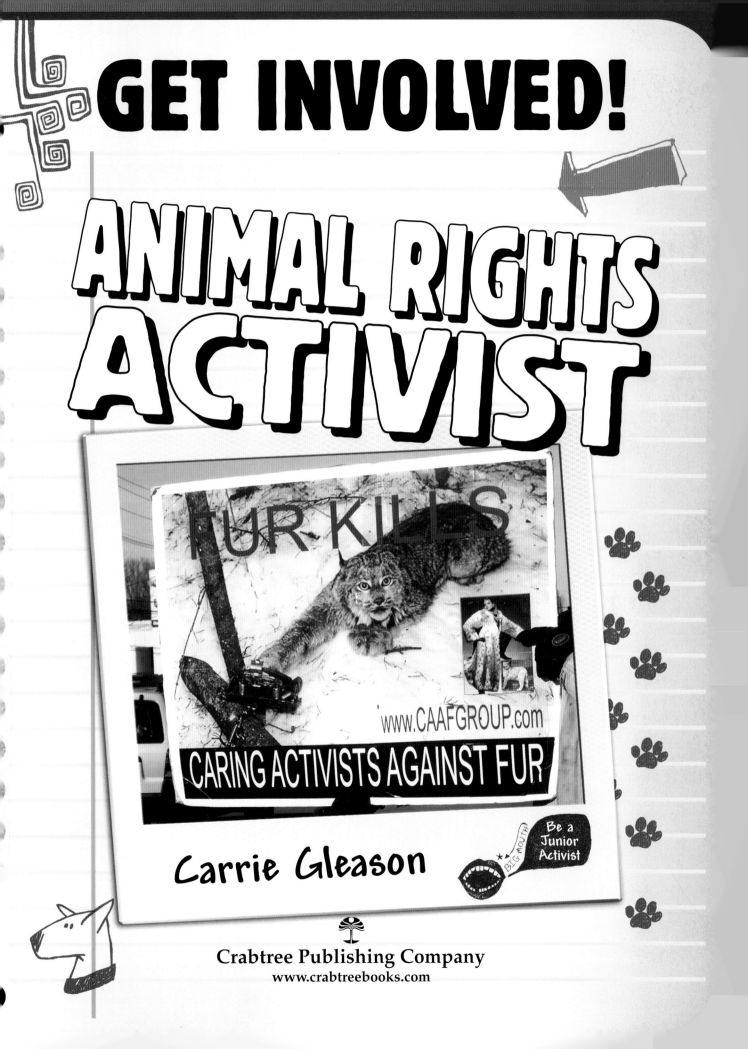

FUR KILLS

www.CAAFGROUP.com

CARING ACTIVISTS AGAINST FUR

Be a Junior Activist

BIG MOUTH!

Carrie Gleason

Crabtree Publishing Company
www.crabtreebooks.com

Crabtree Publishing Company

www.crabtreebooks.com

For today's activists, who need to know and remember the past in order to make a better tomorrow.

Developed and produced by Plan B Book Packagers

Author:
Carrie Gleason

Art director:
Rosie Gowsell-Pattison

Editorial Director:
Ellen Rodger

Production Coordinator:
Margaret Amy Salter

Editor:
Molly Aloian

Proofreader:
Adrianna Morganelli

Photographs:
Alamy: Hugh Sturrock: front cover
Corbis: Kennan Ward: p. 26; Peter Andrews: p. 27
Plan B: Tank: p. 5 (bottom); Newton: p. 28 (top)
Shutterstock: luminouslens: cover (paper); Susan Kehoe: p. 1; roadk:
   p. 3; Susan Kehoe: p. 4 (top); Oshchepkov Dmitry: p. 4 (bottom);
   Johanna Goodyear: p. 5 (top); Adam Gasson: p. 6 (both); Andy
   Lim: p. 7; Sergey Petrov: p. 8 (left); R. Gino Santa Maria:
   p. 8 (right); Tyler Olson: p. 9 (top); Natalia Mikhaylova:
   p. 9 (bottom); Efremova Irina: p. 10 (bottom); Cathleen
   Clapper: p. 10 (top); Eric Isselée: p. 11 (bottom), 18 (top);
   Helmut Konrad Watson: p. 11 (top); Paul Cowan: p. 12 (bottom);
   Grigory Kubatyan: p. 12 (top); Jose AS Reyes: p. 13;

Maslov Dmitry: p. 14 (top); Daniel Gale: p. 14 (bottom); Ragne
Kabanova: p. 14 (middle); Helen Von Allmen: p. 15; Jeremy
Richards: p. 16 (top); Marc van Vuren: p. 16 (bottom); Iofoto:
p. 17 (top); Marafona: p. 17 (bottom); Ngo Thye Aun:
p. 18 (bottom); Charlene Bayerle: p. 19; Bianda Ahmad Hisham:
p. 20 (bottom), 21; Thoma: p. 20 (top); Eky Chan: p. 22 (top);
Sergey Petrov: p. 22 (bottom); Absolut: p. 23 (top); Denis Pepin:
p. 23 (bottom); Ron Hilton: p. 24; FloridaStock: p. 25; Ronnie
Howard: p. 28 (bottom); Wayne Johnson: p. 29; Crystal Kirk: p. 31

Field Notes credits:
p. 7: Ingrid Newkirk quote courtesy of the Home Box Office (HBO)
film *I AM AN ANIMAL: The Life & Work of Ingrid Newkirk*.; p. 13:
"What Constitutes Animal Cruelty" Copyright © 2008. The American
Society for the Prevention of Cruelty to Animals (ASPCA). All Rights
Reserved.; p. 17: Alison Hansen-Decelles quotation courtesy of the
Humane Society of the United States (www.humanesociety.org/youth);
p. 25: Seal hunt activist quote courtesy of the International Fund for
Animal Welfare.; p. 29: Stephanie Cohen quotation courtesy of the
Humane Society of the United States (www.humanesociety.org/youth).

Cover: An orangutan is held in captivity for commercial purposes
after being removed from its natural environment.

Title page: Protestors with handmade signs gather together as
one group on the steps of a public building.

Publisher's note to teachers and parents
Although careful consideration has been made in selecting the list
of Web sites, due to the nature of the subjects' content some Web
sites may contain or have a link to content and images of a sensitive
nature. The views and opinions presented in these Web sites are
those of the organization and do not represent the views and policies
of Crabtree Publishing. As Web site content and addresses often
change, Crabtree Publishing accepts no liability for the content
of the Web sites.

Library and Archives Canada Cataloguing in Publication

Gleason, Carrie, 1973-
   Animal rights activist / Carrie Gleason.

(Get involved!)
Includes index.
ISBN 978-0-7787-4693-5 (bound).--ISBN 978-0-7787-4705-5 (pbk.)

   1. Animal rights activists--Juvenile literature. 2. Animal
rights--Juvenile literature. 3. Animal welfare--Juvenile literature.
I. Title. II. Series: Get involved!

HV4708.G54 2010   j179'.3   C2009-901929-9

Library of Congress Cataloging-in-Publication Data

Gleason, Carrie.
   Animal rights activist / Carrie Gleason.
      p. cm. -- (Get involved!)
   Includes index.
   ISBN 978-0-7787-4705-5 (pbk. : alk. paper) -- ISBN 978-0-7787-4693-5 (reinforced
library binding : alk. paper)
   1. Animal rights activists--United States--Juvenile literature. 2. Animal rights--United
States--Vocational guidance--Juvenile literature. 3. Animal welfare--United States--
Juvenile literature. I. Title. II. Series.

HV4764.G54 2010
179'.3--dc22
                                         2009013134

Crabtree Publishing Company

Published in Canada	**Published in the United States**	**Published in the United Kingdom**	**Published in Australia**
Crabtree Publishing	**Crabtree Publishing**	**Crabtree Publishing**	**Crabtree Publishing**
616 Welland Ave.	PMB16A	White Cross Mills	386 Mt. Alexander Rd.
St. Catharines, ON	350 Fifth Ave., Suite 3308	High Town, Lancaster	Ascot Vale (Melbourne)
L2M 5V6	New York, NY 10118	LA1 4XS	VIC 3032

Contents

GET INVOLVED!

What are animal rights?

An activist is someone who stands up and speaks out for those who cannot speak for themselves. These animal rights activists are protesting the use of animal fur in fashions by holding up posters of skinned animals.

Does the sound and sight of a whimpering puppy in a cage make your heart melt? Do you pause to think that the meat you are about to eat was once a living animal? Are you disturbed by the thought of wearing clothing or boots made from animal skins? If so, animal rights activism may be a cause for you to get involved in.

Treating animals kindly

People who take action to make sure that animals are treated kindly are called animal welfare activists. They feel that animals should be respected and not harmed. Some people take this belief even further. They feel that animals should have the same rights as people. Denying animals these rights is called speciesism, and is an **injustice** like racism or sexism. These people are animal rights activists.

What are rights?

All humans have basic rights and freedoms known as human rights. For example, people believe two basic rights are equality and freedom. Animal rights activists believe that all animals should have the same rights as humans. They believe it is not **ethical**, or right, to treat animals as property or objects. Animal rights activists are against keeping animals in cages, or using them for scientific experiments, or entertainment. Some do not believe it is ethical to own a pet because this denies them their freedom.

Get Active!

Is it right to own a pet?

Do you have a pet? What do you think your pet does all day while you are at school? Some animal rights activists argue that your pet is being kept prisoner in your home. They believe that animals should be liberated, or freed. Do you agree?

Take a look at all the different animals we keep as pets. Where are they kept? What are they fed? Does this seem natural to you? Do you have an ant farm? If so, here is your first step to being an animal rights activist: take it outside and free the ants.

5

What is an activist?

Activists are people who speak up about a cause they believe in. Activists use many different methods to bring about change, such as protests, marches, and rallies. These events bring together large numbers of people who believe in the same cause at a set time and place. A large gathering like this draws the attention of people passing by.

Activists get extra attention by holding up signs with slogans on them, or giving speeches and singing chants. This draws awareness to their cause. Sometimes, a celebrity will give a talk at a protest, drawing media interest and fans.

Celebrity support is an effective way to get the message of activists to a larger audience. Musical artists Pink (top) and Morrisey (bottom) are outspoken animal rights activists.

Methods for change

One common method activists use is a boycott. For animal rights activists, this means not shopping at stores that sell clothing or other goods made from animal skins or furs. Other simple but powerful methods that lead to change are writing letters, making pamphlets, and posting **Internet blogs** to make others aware. Some activists join organizations that support their causes. The ultimate goal in all of these actions is to pressure governments, businesses, and others in society to change.

Field Notes:

Activists believe it is their moral or ethical duty to defend animals. Morals are what a person believes to be right or wrong. Everyone has slightly different morals. Co-founder and president of People for the Ethical Treatment of Animals (PETA), Ingrid Newkirk, explains here what drove her to form the largest animal rights organization in the world.

"For my whole adult life I've felt absolutely driven to try to convince people to consider animals — no matter what they are doing, whether they are buying something to eat or wear, or they've got a dog in their house. They need to think of what that animal is going through, to put that animal in the equation.

It matters to me. I don't know why. I didn't choose it. It might just be purely that I can imagine myself going through exactly what they're going through, and I want to stop it."

HBO

The event that changed activist Ingrid Newkirk's life was working in an animal shelter. This is where she started reading about animal rights.

Welfare or rights?

Most people agree that it is not right to make an animal suffer. But this is where the agreement between animal welfare activists and animal rights activists usually ends.

Animal welfare

Animal welfare activists work to ensure that animals are well looked after and are given food and shelter. They want to make sure that animals are not treated cruelly. At the same time, many animal welfare activists believe it is okay to eat meat and use products, such as clothing, made from animals.

Animal rights

Animal rights activists work to stop the suffering of animals as well as the killing and **exploiting** of animals for any human use.

How would you feel if someone kept you in a cage and forced you to do tricks for crowds of people? Animal rights activists say circuses that use animal acts are unethical.

ts
t, but
ed
.

What do you believe?

tions to determine whether you are
ts, or an animal welfare, supporter:
of a zoo is okay as long as the animals
rly?
g shows should be allowed?
y to use animals in television shows and movies as long as they are treated right? Do you think animals should be used in circuses? Do you eat meat or foods with animal products in them? Do you support hunting? Animal rights activists answer "no" to all of the above. They object to all uses of animals under any circumstances. Animal rights activists believe that animal welfare is part of the problem.

An animal rights activist takes to the stage at a fashion show to call attention to the use of fur in high fashion.

History of animal use

Humans have depended on animals for over two million years for their meat, skins, and furs. Some cultures today still depend heavily on hunting animals for survival.

Traditionally, the **Inuit** of the Canadian Arctic hunted seals and other marine animals. They eat seal meat, use its fat for oil, and its skin for clothing. Without the seal hunt, they would never have survived in the harsh Arctic environment. Seal and other Arctic animals are still a part of the Inuit diet today.

Before powered farm machinery was common, horses were used to pull wagons and assist with farmwork.

Domesticating animals

Humans began farming about 10,000 years ago. They **domesticated** animals to help them with this work. In some cultures today, people still rely heavily on domesticated animals. In the mountains of Tibet and Pakistan, people depend on yaks for their meat, milk, and wool, and to carry heavy loads. These animals are strong and can easily move on the rocky mountain terrain where vehicles cannot go.

Mountain peoples in central Asia herd yaks, which supply them with almost everything they need to survive.

Views on animals

Religion has played an important role in how we view animals. Religious views often determine whether people think of animals as equals or as lesser beings. The Christian holy book, the Bible, says humans should have dominion, or rule, over other living things.

In many religions, including Hinduism, all living creatures have souls. Cattle are considered sacred and are not killed for meat.

In Judaism and Islam, there are very strict rules about which animals can be slaughtered for their meat and how. In many traditional eastern and Asian religions, people learn to respect all animals. Some even teach that it is wrong to harm or kill animals for their meat, eggs, or milk.

Animal cruelty laws

The first animal cruelty laws were passed in England and America in the early 1600s. These laws often protected the rights of the owners of the animals, and not the animals themselves. Cockfighting, dogfighting, and bullbaiting, where dogs were bred and trained to fight bulls, were popular betting sports. The animals were often killed or horribly maimed for entertainment. It was not until 1822 when the world's first animal protection law was passed, in England. It was followed by an 1876 law against cruelty to animals.

Dogs were bred and trained to fight.

By the mid-1800s, some people wondered whether animals should have rights, too.

Bringing about change

The Society for the Prevention of Cruelty to Animals (which later became the RSPCA) was established in a coffee house called Old Slaughter's in London, England, in 1824. Its members tried to stop people from being cruel to farm animals. In 1832, 181 people were charged with cruelty against animals because of the society's investigations.

People as animals

In the mid-1800s, published works by English **naturalist** Charles Darwin began to challenge established ideas about where humans came from and their relationship to the animal kingdom. Darwin's works suggested that humans evolved from apes. People began to wonder what set humans apart from animals. They began to wonder: if people have rights, and they are animals, does that mean that other animals have rights, too?

Field Notes:

The Society for the Prevention of Cruelty to Animals has spread to many countries outside England where it was first started. SPCA officers in the United States and Canada have the authority under law to investigate reports of animal cruelty and to remove animals from these situations. The SPCA depends on tips of animal cruelty given to them by the public. Here, according to the American Society for the Prevention of Cruelty to Animals (ASPCA) are some signs that an animal is being mistreated.

* Tick or flea infestations
* Wounds on the body
* Patches of missing hair
* Extremely thin, starving animal
* Limping
* An owner striking or otherwise physically abusing an animal
* Dogs who are repeatedly left alone without food and water, and often chained in a yard
* Dogs who have been hit by cars—or are showing any of the signs listed here—and have not been taken to a veterinarian
* Dogs who are kept outside without shelter in extreme weather conditions
* Animals who cower in fear or act aggressively when approached by their owners

Birth of animal rights

People have been using animals in medical research for thousands of years. The ancient Greeks performed surgery on living animals to learn about **anatomy**. This kind of experimentation is known as vivisection.

Many scientific and medical discoveries were made by scientists who experimented on and killed animals. In the mid-1800s, groups of activists opposed to animal experimentation began to pressure researchers and governments to stop the practice. These activists were called antivivisectionists.

Many labs use animals to test new drugs or products.

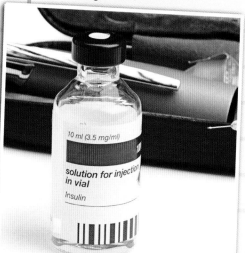

Antivivisection activists

In Britain, antivivisectionists pressed the government to pass a Cruelty to Animals Act in 1876. The act was a compromise: antivivisectionists wanted to end all animal experimentation while researchers argued that it was necessary to advance science. The act forced researchers experimenting on animals to follow rules. It became a model for animal protection laws in other countries.

After World War II, the number of animals used in laboratories for testing and the size of animal farms rose. A 1952 law in the United States stated that all cats and dogs belonging to publicly funded animal shelters be donated for medical research. Many people spoke out against this, and some shelters gave up the funding so they could keep the animals. Activists lobbied the government for laws that better protected animals.

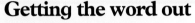

Getting the word out

In England in the late 1960s, a group of university **philosophers** started to talk about the rights of animals. They published articles in newspapers and books. One book called *Animal Liberation* published by Australian Peter Singer in 1975 greatly influenced activists. Singer argued that humans and animals were different but all animals can suffer, and should therefore be given equal consideration. Although Singer's ideas might not seem **radical** to us today, at the time they were shocking and made many people change their way of thinking about animals.

A 1970s cartoon depicted Singer as a peace lover.

Get Active!

Rights vs. welfare research

What's the difference between an animal rights, and an animal welfare, organization? The SPCA is an animal welfare organization. People for the Ethical Treatment of Animals, or PETA, is an animal rights organization. Using the Internet, research these two organizations as well as the ones listed on pages 30-31 of this book. What are the differences between them? What are the similarities? (Warning: Some Web sites show explicit images of animal cruelty that you might not be comfortable seeing. Have a parent or other adult check the sites first).

Vegetarianism

The average person will eat 1,000 chickens, 30 sheep, and 20 pigs in their lifetime. But not vegetarians, or people who refuse to eat meat.

Almost three percent of Americans and four percent of Canadians today are vegetarian. There are many reasons. Some object to modern farming practices, or are worried about the quality of meat. Others believe vegetarianism is better for the environment.

Veganism

Most animal rights activists believe it is unethical to eat or use the flesh of animals. They follow a vegan lifestyle that does not use animals for food, clothing, or any other purpose.

Vegans do not eat eggs or dairy products, such as cheese, milk, or ice cream, or desserts and candies that contain gelatin, which is made from animal bones. Vegans use vegetable oils as alternatives to lard, or pig fat, which is traditionally used in baking. Vegans do not wear wool, leather, or silk clothing and do what they can to prevent animal suffering.

Some cultures do not eat meat and follow vegetarian or vegan diets.

Vegans believe many people forget that the meat they eat once had a face.

Field Notes:

High school student Alison Hansen-Decelles became active in a campaign started by another student to convince her school cafeteria to offer vegetarian and vegan meals to the students. Here, in Alison's own words, is why she made the choice to become a vegetarian.

I LOVE VEGANS

"I became an ethical vegetarian at five after finding out that animals are killed specifically to produce meat. My thinking was very simplistic then: you don't kill animals if you can help it. When I was fifteen, I stumbled into Peter Singer's Animal Liberation and went vegan. I realized that animal abuse is an injustice like any other, even though it crosses the species barrier. If it can be recognized as an injustice, it has an end in sight. Maybe hundreds of years down the road, but the case is there, and it's sound."

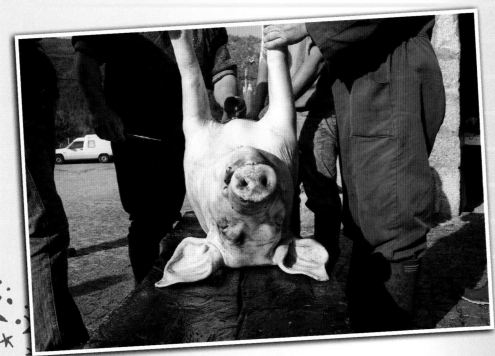

Animal testing

Animals, such as rats, mice, guinea pigs, hamsters, gerbils, cats, dogs, and monkeys, are used as test subjects in laboratories. Before products, such as makeup, drugs, and household cleaners, are sold to the public, they must by law be tested to make sure they are safe for human use.

In the name of science

People also use animals to find cures and learn more about diseases. Often, they are given diseases that will cause them great pain and eventually kill them. Animal testing has helped scientists develop vaccines and drugs to treat diseases. Surgeries and life-saving equipment for premature babies have also been developed using animal testing.

Is it worth it?

Scientists who support animal testing argue that more can be found out from a test on animals than any other method. Rats for example, breed five times as fast as humans so the tests can tell of any results over many generations faster than using human test subjects. Animal rights activists say that computers can and should be used instead to do these tests, or that a single human cell will also work. They also argue that animals are different species than humans and that many tests show a different result on humans.

Throughout the 1970s and 1980s, U.S. scientists did tests using macaque monkeys.

Field Notes:

English philosopher Jeremy Bentham (1748-1832) was an early animal rights **advocate**. In the 1700s and 1800s, many people argued that animals could not reason or think like humans and this gave humans the right to treat them as things. They could therefore be mistreated or killed at will. But Bentham wrote that the ability to reason should not be a measurement or deciding factor for cruelty. His ideas influenced many later animal rights activists, particularly activists who oppose testing on animals.

"...What else is it that should trace the insuperable (impossible) line? Is it the faculty of reason or perhaps the faculty of discourse (speech)? But a full-grown horse or dog is beyond comparison a more rational, as well as more conversable animal, than an infant of a day, or a week, or even a month old. But suppose they were otherwise, what would it avail? The question is not can they reason, nor can they talk, but can they suffer?"
-Jeremy Bentham, *An Introduction to the Principles of Morals and Legislation.*

Factory farming

Farmers are under pressure from consumers to keep meat prices low. Some farms have developed into enormous "factory farms." To save money, these farms raise thousands of animals using less time and space than smaller family farms. The animals are treated more like goods manufactured in a factory than living things.

Cattle are kept on feedlots where they are fattened before they are slaughtered. Some feedlots are enormous and crowded.

Animal life

Animal rights activists oppose factory farming for a number of reasons. Animals, such as chickens or hogs, are kept indoors in small cages or pens that are often too small for them to move around in or lay down. They are not allowed outside for exercise. Activists say that this is cruel and gives the animals a poor quality of life.

Animals kept in small spaces often develop joint pain. Hens are kept in cages so small that they cannot lift their wings. Chickens often become distressed and violent when confined in small spaces. To avoid having the animals peck at each other, their beaks are often cut or burned off.

Free range chickens are allowed to roam free.

Five freedoms

In 1964, an animal welfare activist in Britain published a book that revealed the reality of factory farming. The book made many people aware of these farming practices. As a result, the British government set up a committee to investigate. They came up with a list of "five freedoms"—a number of recommendations for the treatment of farm animals. Now, other countries also use this formula to develop **policies** regarding animal welfare on farms. The five freedoms that animals should have are:

- Freedom from thirst and hunger
- Freedom from discomfort
- Freedom from pain, injury, and disease
- Freedom to express normal behavior
- Freedom from fear and distress.

Get Active!   Down on the farm

Some animal welfare activists reject meat from animals that had been raised on factory farms. Instead, they look for meat that is labeled "organic" or "free range." Look into what these two terms mean. Who regulates the use of these terms in your area? How do you know if you are getting what you think you are getting when you buy these products?

Fighting cruelty

Cruelty to animals means causing unnecessary pain and suffering to them. Animal shelters are bombarded with calls about pets who have been beaten, neglected, or abandoned by their owners. These animals are taken to shelters where they are cared for until they are adopted. If no one adopts them, some shelters "put them to sleep," or kill them using an injection of drugs. Shelters want people to do research before buying a pet to make sure that they are aware of the work and responsibility involved.

Caging animals for long periods of time makes them suffer.

Working animals

Animals perform all kinds of jobs for humans. Guide dogs are trained to be the "eyes" of blind people. Dogs are also trained to be used in police forces and the army. They are used to detect drugs and bombs. Some dogs are trained to be guard dogs. Herding dogs are used on farms to control livestock. Many other animals are used for work, including horses, donkeys, and camels.

Animal welfare activists try to ensure working animals are treated well.

Animal welfare activists believe it is not wrong to use an animal for these purposes, as long as the animal is not mistreated. Animal rights activists object to this, saying that they are being trained to go against their natural instincts.

Bulls are killed after being taunted and stabbed during bullfights.

Blood sports

In nature, animals fight with one another for territory, food, or mates. In **captivity**, some animals are bred for fighting to amuse a human audience. These types of activities are called blood sports. Examples of blood sports are bullfighting, dogfighting, and cockfighting. Animal rights activists consider hunting to be a blood sport as well.

Animals in cages

Animal rights activists think it is wrong to keep animals in cages. They object to keeping animals as pets and to animals being trained and used in any form of entertainment such as movies, circuses, and shows.

Would dogs naturally dress up and perform for an audience?

Get Active!

What is cruelty?

Investigate animal welfare and cruelty laws in your state or province. What do they say? Do you think they go far enough in protecting animals from cruel treatment? If not, write a letter to your government urging them to strengthen animal welfare legislation. Get your friends, family, neighbors, and classmates to write, too!

Animals on screen

Animals have been used in movies and television for many years. In the early days of movies, there were no regulations and animals sometimes died when performing dangerous stunts. The American Humane Association (AHA) now monitors film and television productions made in the United States to make sure animals who work are not harmed. The AHA also produces guidelines for animal safety in films and rates movies for their level of protection.

Animal rights activists believe rodeos are cruel. Many animal rights organizations mount campaigns to end rodeos by publicizing examples of cruelty and by pressuring corporate sponsors to stop giving money to the rodeos.

Field Notes:

Each spring, the Canadian seal hunt takes place off the northeast coast of Canada. Hundreds of thousands of seals are killed during this time. Most are adolescent harp seals. Until 1987, young harp seal pups were also killed for their white fur. In 1987, under pressure from animal rights activists, the International Fund for Animal Welfare (IFAW), the clubbing to death or shooting of seal pups was banned by the Canadian government. Today, the IFAW questions the methods used by seal hunters. Here is a quote from an IFAW activist about the seal hunt:

"I saw animals being shot from boats and injured; these young seals were not killed quickly or humanely. . . One animal was crawling around on the ice bleeding for over a minute before the boat arrived and a sealer jumped down onto the ice pan to kill it with a club. It never ceases to amaze me that sealers see a seal crawling around on the ice suffering, yet they don't act quickly and shoot the animal again to put it out of its misery . . . What we document out here is unacceptable and the world needs to see what only a few people have the ability to view in person. IFAW is here to document the hunt so that the world can see that this hunt is inherently cruel and is not monitored or enforced like the government claims."

In the trenches

Many famous animal activists have been mentioned earlier in this book such as Ingrid Newkirk and Peter Singer. But there are many more champions of animal rights. There are also millions of people around the world who fight and support animal rights and welfare every day.

Henry Spira

Henry Spira was a Belgian-born immigrant to the United States. In 1974, he formed Animal Rights International after being inspired by Peter Singer. Two years later, Spira took **direct action** against the Museum of Natural History in New York by protesting outside their doors on experiments they were doing on cats. Spira's efforts paid off. After eighteen months, the experiments were stopped. Spira also took action against a cosmetics company for testing on rabbits, which ended up blinding them.

Jane Goodall travels the world to speak about protecting animals.

Jane Goodall

Some activists choose to help one animal in particular. An example of this is **primatologist** Jane Goodall. Goodall became interested in apes as a child when she received a chimpanzee toy. As an adult, she went to a jungle in Tanzania, Africa, to study wild chimpanzees in their natural habitat. Goodall's decades of observation and devotion to primates taught people many things about them. As part of her life-long dedication to the welfare of the animals she loves, she started the Jane Goodall Institute in 1977.

Alicia Silverstone

Alicia Silverstone is one of several Hollywood stars, including Pamela Anderson and Eva Mendes, who use their celebrity status to promote animal welfare and rights causes. A vegan and supporter of the animal protection group PETA, Silverstone has taken part in PETA's anti-fur advertising campaigns. She also speaks publicly about animal rights and encourages others to follow vegetarian or vegan diets.

Alicia Silverstone uses her fame to promote animal rights causes.

Tom Regan

American philosopher Tom Regan argues that we grant rights to humans who are mentally ill and to infants who cannot speak for themselves, so why not to animals? Regan has said that "the truth of animal rights requires empty cages, not larger cages." He is the author of several books on animal rights.

Paul Watson

Paul Watson is a Canadian animal rights activist and environmentalist. In 1975, while protesting Russian whaling ships with environmental group Greenpeace, Watson states that looking into the eye of a dying whale changed him forever. He formed a direct action group called Sea Shepherd that protests against whaling and sealing, using actions such as ramming whaling ships.

What you can do

There are many things you can do as an animal welfare or animal rights activist. You can start by changing the way you live. Refusing to wear clothing or shoes made of animal furs or leather is an easy place to start. Read the labels of cosmetics and household products, and make sure they say "not tested on animals" on their labels. Vegetarianism or veganism is another personal change you can make.

Taking it further

If you have some spare time, you can offer to become involved in animal welfare. Something as simple as offering to walk your own or your neighbor's pets makes sure that the animals get plenty of fresh air and exercise, which are essential for their health. You can also offer to volunteer at an animal shelter. Animal shelters need people to help raise funds and awareness.

BIG MOUTH

Get Active!

Awareness exercise

Think of ways to raise awareness of an animal in danger. To raise funds for donation, here are some ideas to get you started:
- make magnets to sell that picture the animal you want to help
- design a T-shirt with a logo that features the animal and take orders for them
- make holiday, birthday, or get-well cards that feature your animal with a message inside about your cause and sell them

Field Notes:

Stephanie Cohen was a child when she became involved in a program to protect animals. Through hard work and determination, her efforts grew into a non-profit organization called Kids Making a Difference. The organization supports programs started by kids to benefit their communities, whether it be cleaning up streets or fostering homeless pets. The organizations's motto is "Saving Our World One Animal at a Time." Here's how Stephanie got started:

"When I was in the second grade, I read a newspaper article about an injured baby manatee. It was then that I decided that I wanted to do something, and I did. I started making manatee pins and selling them to family and friends to raise money and public awareness for these gentle giants. As kids heard of my efforts, they too became interested and wanted to get involved. Being a lover of all animals and wanting to expand my efforts, in 2003 I formed Kids Making A Difference."

Saving the animals

On this page, you will find Web sites of some well-known organizations that appear in this book. It is important that you view these sites with your teacher or parent. Some Web sites or links from these sites may contain topics and images of a sensitive nature. Discuss the information you read on these Web sites with your teacher or parent, and then make up your own mind about how you feel about the subject.

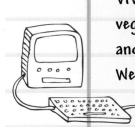

Animal Welfare Institute (AWI):

AWI began as an organization to save animals used in laboratory tests. They have also worked to reduce the pain that people cause to animals through factory farming. www.awionline.org

Vegetarians International Voice for Animals (VIVA):

VIVA is an organization started in the UK for all people interested in becoming vegetarian or vegan for animal rights. VIVA has information on animal farming and recipes for getting started with a vegetarian lifestyle. The organization's Web site for young people is www.vivaactivists.org.uk.

People for the Ethical Treatment of Animals (PETA):

With more than two million members, PETA claims to be the world's largest animal rights organization. PETA's Web site has animal rights news and information on how to get active and live cruelty-free. Their Web site for young people is www.petakids.com.

Society for the Prevention of Cruelty to Animals (SPCA):

There are branches of the SPCA all over the world. These are shelters that take care of abandoned and abused animals. They are usually looking for people to volunteer their time in the shelter or for fundraising. Check out your local phone book for the branch nearest you.

Humane Society of the United States (HSUS) and of Canada (HSC):

The HSUS is the world's largest animal welfare and advocacy group with over seven million members. Their purpose is to protect animals from cruelty and neglect. They also serve to educate the community about animal welfare and protect wildlife habitats.

In the United States, visit the Humane Society at www.hsus.org, and, in Canada, visit www.humanesociety.com.

GET ACTIVE!

Glossary

advocate Someone who publicly supports a cause or plan of action

anatomy A branch of science that studies bodily structures

captivity Imprisoned or confined

direct action Action taken by individuals or groups to make social change. Examples of direct action include strikes, protests, and sit-ins

domesticate To tame an animal or keep it for agricultural purposes

ethical Concerned with what is right and wrong

exploit To use and benefit unfairly from someone or something else

injustice Lack of fairness

Internet blog A Web site that a person or organization uses to speak about issues or ideas

Inuit The indigenous people of the Arctic in Canada, parts of Greenland, and Alaska

naturalist Someone who studies the natural world

philosopher Someone who studies and writes about knowledge and ideas

policy A course of action followed by a government, a business, or an organization

primatologist A scientist who studies primates, such as chimpanzees, monkeys, and apes

radical Something that departs from what is considered normal or traditional

Index

Printed in China — CT